MISSION
BARCELONA

Author: Catherine Aragon
Designer: Nada Orlić • Content Editor: Sue Peterson

CONTENTS:

AFTER COMPLETING EACH MISSION CHECK (√) THE BOX AND WRITE THE NUMBER OF POINTS EARNED.

AT THE END, WRITE THE TOTAL NUMBER OF POINTS HERE:

ATTENTION: FUTURE SPECIAL AGENTS <u>YOU</u>
AND CASE OFFICERS <u>GROWNUPS</u>

CONGRATULATIONS! THE SIA (SECRET INTERNATIONAL AGENCY) HAS SELECTED YOU AS A CANDIDATE TO BECOME A SPECIAL AGENT.

The SIA carries out important assignments, secretly collecting intelligence in all corners of the globe. ("Intelligence" is spy-speak for "information.") Currently, we are in dire need of agents. Many want to join us, but only a few have what it takes.

HOW WILL YOU PROVE YOU'RE READY TO JOIN THE MOST ELITE SPY AGENCY IN THE WORLD? You must complete a series of missions in Barcelona. Similar to a scavenger hunt (only better), these missions will require you to carry out challenging investigations and collect valuable intel (short for "intelligence"). For each mission, you'll earn points towards becoming a special agent.

YOUR ASSIGNMENT: TRAVEL TO BARCELONA WITH YOUR TEAM, LED BY YOUR CASE OFFICER. (A case officer accompanies agents on missions. Your case officer is your parent or other trusted adult.) You must earn at least 100 points to become a SIA special agent.

-The mission list and mission scorecard are on page 1.

-Read the "Anytime Missions" early, so that you'll remain on alert and ready to earn points.

-You don't need to complete all of the missions to reach 100 points or complete them in any particular order.

MISSION RULES

- Be kind and respectful to team members.

- Your case officer has the final decision regarding point awards.

- Your case officer serves as the official "scorekeeper."

- Your case officer has the final decision on what missions will be attempted. (Don't worry, you can still earn enough points to become an agent without completing all the missions.)

- Always be on alert. You never know when a chance to earn points lies just around the corner.

TO CONCEAL THEIR REAL IDENTITIES, SPECIAL AGENTS ALWAYS USE CODE NAMES. FOR EXAMPLE, JAMES BOND'S CODE NAME IS 007. THINK OF YOUR OWN CODE NAME TO USE DURING YOUR MISSION IN BARCELONA.

SIGN YOUR CODE NAME HERE:

Anni

———————————
DATE

IMPORTANT: FOR THE MISSIONS YOU WILL NEED A PEN OR PENCIL AND A CAMERA.

LET THE MISSIONS BEGIN - GOOD LUCK!

AGENTS MUST HAVE SHARP SKILLS WHEN IT COMES TO ANALYZING IMAGES, SUCH AS PHOTOS, IN ORDER TO GATHER IMPORTANT INTEL.

"Intel" is short for "intelligence." Aerial photos like this one are taken from high in the sky by a satellite, a machine that orbits the Earth and takes pictures. Governments sometimes use satellites for spying, and other times simply for gathering information.

A satellite snapped this photo of Europe at night. The clusters of white light are night-time city lights.

1- Spain 2- Portugal 3- France 4- United Kingdom 5- Ireland
6- Netherlands 7- Belgium 8- Germany 9- Switzerland
10- Italy 11- Morocco 12- Algeria 13- Tunisia

Look at the outlines of Spain using the map, and then try to make out Spain in the satellite photo. Next, look at the location of Barcelona on the map. Then…

☐ **FIND BARCELONA ON THE SATELLITE PHOTO AND CIRCLE IT.** (Remember, large cities like Barcelona will have the most lights.)

1 POINT

AGENTS MUST SPEAK FOREIGN LANGUAGES, TO BLEND IN WHEREVER THEIR MISSIONS TAKE THEM.

In Barcelona, things get a little tricky because many people speak two languages. Barcelona is part of Spain. People speak Spanish and a language called "Catalan." Catalan is similar to Spanish and unique to this part of the country.

We don't expect you to magically become fluent in Spanish or Catalan overnight. However here are a few key words you must know. Can you find any words in Spanish that are similar to Catalan?

English	Spanish	pronunciation	Catalan	pronunciation
Hello	Hola	"Oh-la"	Hola	"Oh-la"
Goodbye	Adiós	"Ah-dee-os"	Adéu	"Ah-day-oo"
Yes	Sí	"See"	Sí	"See"
No	No	"No"	No	"No"
Please	Por favor	"Pore-fa-vore"	Si us plau	"See-oos-plow"
Thank you	Gracias	"Grah-see-as"	Gràcies	"Grah-see-es"

SYMBOLS OF BARCELONA

THE BEST SECRET AGENTS HAVE SOMETHING IN COMMON — THEY ARE ALWAYS ON ALERT.

As you wander around Barcelona, a city filled with symbols scattered throughout its streets, squares and sights, remain on alert for two objects in particular: dragons and bats. Here's the lowdown on these two symbols that you must find to complete several of your missions.

The dragon

Hundreds of dragons hide throughout Barcelona. They lurk in sculptures, fountains and monuments. Sometimes the dragons stand alone, other times they defend themselves from attack by a brave knight. This courageous soldier is Jordi, ("Jordee") ("George" in English) the city's patron saint.

Legend has it that around 1700 years ago, an evil dragon resided in a tiny village not far from Barcelona. This vile creature destroyed everything, ate all the animals in the small town, and eventually began feasting on the villagers themselves.

Each day a new person was sacrificed to the dragon. Finally, the village's princess was selected for sacrifice. The monster was just about to devour the princess, when a fearless knight by the name of Jordi emerged. He drove his sword into the dragon, thereby saving the princess and killing the beast. And on the spot where the dragon's blood fell, a red rose bush grew.

Nowadays, the image of Saint Jordi and the dragon appears all around the city, and on April 23 (the day that Saint Jordi died in the year 303), every man in Barcelona gives his darling a red rose.

The bat

In the 13th century, King Jaume I ("Jham") ("James" in English) ruled the city as the Count of Barcelona.

King Jaume spent much of his time on the battlefield, always attempting to conquer more territory for his kingdom of Aragon. The night before King Jaume and his men were to fight a crucial battle to win the valuable

lands of Valencia for Aragon, King Jaume's nerves were getting the best of him. Usually his men fully supported him, but this time they didn't back his battle plans. The king began to question himself, and the last thing he needed before an important fight was doubt. Instead of feeling pumped up and confident, he felt confused and nervous.

According to legend, late that night, just before the king fell asleep, a bat flew into his tent. Then, while asleep, the king dreamed of victory. In the morning, his worries were but distant memory – he was 100% certain that he and his men must push forward to claim Valencia. They won the battle! As for the bat, which King Jaume took for a powerful omen, it became a symbol of Barcelona.

LA RAMBLA

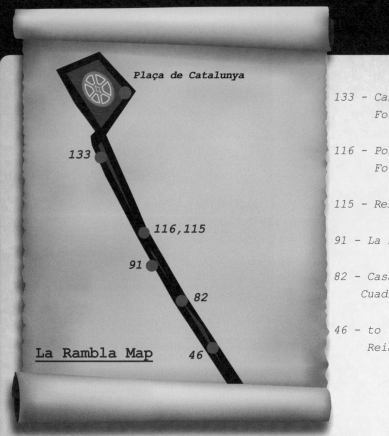

Plaça de Catalunya

133 - Canaletes
      Fountain

116 - Portaferrissa
      Fountain

115 - Reial Acadèmia

91 - La Boqueria

82 - Casa Bruno
     Cuadros

46 - to the Plaça
     Reial

133

116,115

91

82

La Rambla Map   46

This mission will put your map-reading skills to the test.

Use this map to uncover each of these points along La Rambla, a one-mile walk along Barcelona's most famous street.

AGENTS MUST HAVE A KEEN EYE FOR DETAILS — A CRITICAL SKILL WHEN GATHERING INTELLIGENCE.

Keep your eyes peeled for clues, as well as pickpockets. La Rambla is a hot-spot for these thieves attempting to steal wallets, cameras, and mobile phones.

30

TOTAL POINTS

As you walk along La Rambla track down:

☐ **A STREET SIGN LIKE THIS ONE** — 2 POINTS

☐ **AT LEAST FIVE "HUMAN STATUES"** — 2 POINTS

☐ **AT LEAST TWO STATUES PAINTED HEAD-TO-TOE** — 1 POINT

PLAÇA DE CATALUNYA:

(Plaça de Catalunya = "Pla-sa duh Kata-loon-ya")

La Rambla runs from this large, statue-filled square all the way to Barcelona's port.

☐ **LOCATE THIS STATUE.**

2 POINTS

☐ **WHAT DOES SHE HOLD ABOVE HER HEAD?**

1 POINT

This object symbolizes exploration and trade, two activities central to Barcelona's history as a port city.

The statue was sculpted by Frederic M____.

☐ **FIND HIS LAST NAME CARVED INTO THE STATUE FOR THE ANSWER.**

1 POINT

LA RAMBLA, 133: CANALETES FOUNTAIN

(Canaletes = "Ka-na-let-ays")

☐ **HUNT DOWN THE CANALETES FOUNTAIN.** **2 POINTS**

☐ **FIND THE SQUARE PLAQUE WHOSE MESSAGE BEGINS WITH "SI BEVEU AIGUA."** **1 POINT**

In English the message on this plaque means: "if you drink water from the Canaletes Fountain, you'll fall in love with Barcelona forever and, no matter how far away you go, you'll always return."

What do you think? Can drinking water from a special fountain determine your destiny?

☐ **LOCATE THE CITY'S COAT-OF-ARMS ON THE FOUNTAIN. WHICH ONE OF THESE THREE DESIGNS IS THE CITY COAT OF ARMS?** **1 POINT**

a

b

c

LA RAMBLA, 116: PORTAFERRISSA FOUNTAIN

(Portaferrissa = "Port-a-fare-ee-sa")

☐ **TRACK DOWN THE PORTAFERRISSA FOUNTAIN.**

The fountain's tile wall depicts city life hundreds of years ago. Find these things:

☐ **3 DIFFERENT KINDS OF ANIMALS**

☐ **SAINT JOSEPH (HE HOLDS A CROSS AS HE PROTECTS THE CITY.)**

At the Reial Acadèmia de Ciències i Arts (Royal Academy of Sciences and Arts), look up at the clock for Barcelona's official time.

☐ **MAKE SURE THAT THE TIME YOU HAVE IS THE SAME AS THE CITY'S OFFICIAL TIME.**

2 POINTS

(La Boqueria = "Lah Bo-ker-ee-a")

Before venturing into the largest market in Spain, La Boqueria, examine the sign above the entrance.

☐ **WHICH TWO OF THESE ARE NOT ON THE SIGN?**

*An image of Saint Jordi (the city's patron saint)

*The words "Mercat Sant Josep" (the market's official name)

*A bat (a city symbol)

*The Spanish flag (below, right)

*The city's coat of arms (below, left)

☐ **WHAT ARE THE THREE MOST UNUSUAL FOODS YOU CAN FIND INSIDE THE MARKET?**

(Casa Bruno Cuadros = "Ka-sa Broo-no Kwad-rose")

☐ **FIND A CHINESE DRAGON PERCHED ON THE BUILDING'S SECOND FLOOR.** **2** POINTS

Remember the importance of dragons in Barcelona? Today a bank may occupy the building's first floor; but if you look under the dragon, you'll find a clue to this building's original purpose. (It was an umbrella shop.)

☐ **FIND THREE CLOSED UMBRELLA SCULPTURES ON THE OUTSIDE OF THE BUILDING.** **1** POINT

An umbrella will keep you dry, and this accessory will keep you cool.

☐ **UNCOVER THIS ITEM BESIDE THE DRAGON AND DECORATING THE BUILDING'S WALLS. WHAT IS IT?** **1** POINT

☐ **NEAR THE OLD UMBRELLA SHOP, LOCATE THIS MOSAIC.** **1** POINT

A "mosaic" is an image made of small pieces of colored glass or colored stone.

☐ **THE ARTIST JOAN M _____ CREATED THIS MOSAIC.** **1** POINT

Carefully examine the stones to find his last name for the answer. (In Catalan the name Joan *("Jh-wan")* means "John.")

Hunt down La Rambla 46 and go around the corner to arrive at one of the city's most famous squares.

☐ **LOCATE A STREETLAMP WITH TWO OF BARCELONA'S SYMBOLS: THE CITY'S FLAG PAINTED SOMEWHERE ON THE POLE AND DRAGONS TWISTING AROUND THE TOP.**

2 POINTS

THE BEST SECRET AGENTS NEVER FORGET — THEY HAVE KEEN MEMORIES WITH THE ABILITY TO RECALL THE SMALLEST DETAILS ABOUT EVENTS, PEOPLE, AND PLACES.

Now it's time to test yours. On the streetlamp, examine Barcelona's flag and find the red crosses. They're the crosses of Barcelona's male patron saint.

☐ WHOSE CROSSES ARE THESE?

PORT VELL

(Vell = "Vay")

For almost 2,000 years, boats sailing the high seas have called on Barcelona. In Roman times (about 2,000 years ago), when Barcelona was known by a different name, "Barcino," *("Bar-cee-no")* boats would dock here, load up on goods like wine and building materials, and sail across the Mediterranean to the capital Rome, Italy. Today cruiseliners, cargo ships, yachts, and ferries from around the world fill the port. ("Port Vell" means "Old Port.")

- YOUR VESSEL OF CHOICE
- COLUMBUS MONUMENT: PHOTO, COAT-OF-ARMS, BARCELONA + COLON, SEA SYMBOL
- VIEW FROM THE TOP
- OLD CUSTOMS BUILDING
- MODERN ART STATUE
- SANTA EULÀLIA

Before leaving the port, take a stroll around the docks.

☐ WHICH VESSEL WOULD YOU CHOOSE TO TAKE TO THE HIGH SEAS?

2
POINTS

COLUMBUS MONUMENT

Christopher Columbus may have been from Italy, but in 1492 he sailed across the Atlantic Ocean under the Spanish flag. The King and Queen of Spain (Ferdinand and Isabella) were the only ones willing to give him money for his risky voyage in search of unchartered lands. Ferdinand and Isabella's gamble paid off big time, because Columbus claimed lands in the "New World" and brought back riches for Spain. This statue celebrates Columbus' return to Europe, when his ships sailed into the port of Barcelona.

1 POINT ☐ HAVE YOUR PHOTO SNAPPED BENEATH THE MONUMENT POSING LIKE COLUMBUS, POINTING TOWARDS THE OCEAN BLUE.

On the monument locate:

☐ BARCELONA'S COAT OF **1 POINT**
ARMS (THE CROSSES AND
THE STRIPES)

☐ THE WORDS "BARCELONA" **1 POINT**
AND "COLON" TOGETHER
("Colón" means "Columbus" in
Spanish.)

☐ WHAT SYMBOL OF THE SEA **1 POINT**
IS BELOW THESE TWO WORDS?

Venture to the top of the
monument, admire the view,
scan the vista, and find
these landmarks:

☐ HARBOR CLOCK TOWER **1 POINT**

☐ **OLD CUSTOMS BUILDING** `1 POINT`
(Look for "Port de Barcelona"
on this building very near the
statue.)

☐ **MODERN ART STATUE** `1 POINT`

☐ **MONTJUÏC TOWER** `1 POINT`
(Montjuïc = *"Mohn-jhoo-eek"*;
A telecommunications tower used
during the 1992 Olympics to
broadcast events from Barcelona
all around the world.)

**Once you're back on the ground, find these two
structures that you just before spotted from
above:**

☐ **OLD CUSTOMS BUILDING**

☐ **MODERN ART STATUE**
(On the sculpture, can you decipher the face
sticking out from the red dots?)

THE SANTA EULÀLIA

(Eulàlia = "Ew-la-lee-uh")

Named for one of Barcelona's patron saints, the
Santa Eulàlia completed its first voyage in 1918.
("Santa" means "saint.") A few times the ship
completed a roundtrip all the way across the
Atlantic Ocean to Cuba and back.

☐ **HUNT DOWN THIS VESSEL RESTING IN THE
HARBOR.**

(If it's out to sea give yourself an extra point
for finding the old customs building.)

LA CATEDRAL.

(Catedral = "Kah-tay-drahl")

This 700-year-old cathedral was built in memory of one of the city's patron saints, Saint Eulàlia (Eulàlia = "Ew-la-lee-uh"). Eulàlia was born in Barcelona way back in the year 290, when Romans ruled Barcelona. The Romans didn't believe in Christianity and were furious with Eulàlia, a 13-year-old girl who refused their demands that she give up her Christianity. To set an example, the Romans tortured and eventually beheaded Eulàlia. Legend has it that immediately after her beheading, a white dove emerged from her neck.

Inside the cathedral, you'll uncover reminders of Saint Eulàlia.

9

TOTAL POINTS

- THE CRYPT
- COURTYARD BIRDS
- SAINT JORDI FOUNTAIN
- SHOES & SCISSORS SYMBOLS

Saint Eulàlia

☐ FIND THE CRYPT THAT HOLDS HER TOMB.

2 POINTS

In the cloister (the courtyard) live white birds, descendants of a flock calling the cathedral their home for hundreds of years.

You will find 13 here, one for each year of Saint Eulàlia's life.

☐ WHAT KIND OF BIRD ARE THEY?

1 POINT

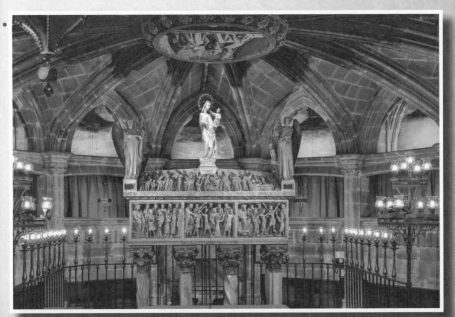

Remember the story of Saint Jordi and the dragon?

☐ **TRACK DOWN THE FOUNTAIN WITH SAINT JORDI MOUNTED UPON HIS HORSE AND SLAYING A DRAGON.**

2 POINTS

When the cathedral was under construction, different trade groups funded small chapels around the courtyard.

These associations left their mark on the cathedral with their group's symbol somewhere on the floor.

KEEP A LOOKOUT UNDER YOUR FEET AND FIND THESE SYMBOLS:

☐ SHOES (THE COBBLERS' GROUP) **2** POINTS

☐ SCISSORS (THE TAILORS' GROUP) **2** POINTS

PLAÇA NOVA

(Plaça Nova = "Pla-sa No-vuh")

This plaza lies just outside the cathedral. Here you'll discover remnants of Barcelona's ancient city wall. The wall dates back to the era when the Romans ruled the city, about 2,000 years ago. Back then, the structure you see today formed part of a massive wall that encircled the whole city, protecting it from enemy attack.

Find Barcelona's Roman name spelled out in the sculpture letters in front of the archways.

☐ **WHAT DID THE ROMANS** **2** POINTS
CALL BARCELONA?

Hunt down this scribbled artwork in the plaza, designed by the famous Spanish artist Pablo Picasso.

☐ **COMPARE THIS COPY TO THE ORIGINAL THAT** **2** POINTS
YOU FIND. UNCOVER ONE ITEM THAT HAS
BEEN ADDED TO THE COPY THAT DOES NOT
APPEAR IN THE ORIGINAL.

PLAÇA DE SANT FELIP NERI

(Plaça de Sant Felip Neri= "Pla-sa duh Sant Fuh-leep Nare-ee")

AGENTS MUST HAVE A KEEN EYE FOR DETAIL.
THEY ALWAYS NEED TO HAVE THEIR EYES
PEELED FOR THE TINIEST CLUES – CRITICAL
INFORMATION THAT OTHERS OFTEN MISS. TIME
TO PUT YOUR SKILLS TO THE TEST.

In this small square, just a quick walk away from
the cathedral, lies a tiny museum of shoes.

☐ ON THE WALL, ABOVE THE **2 POINTS**
MUSEUM'S ENTRANCE, LOCATE THE
SYMBOL OF SAINT MARK, THE PATRON
SAINT OF SHOEMAKERS.

(Look for an animal who's known as the king of
the jungle.)

- SHOEMAKER'S SYMBOL
- SANT FELIP NERI STATUE

my notes:

_____

_____

☐ **LOCATE THIS STATUE LOOKING DOWN OVER THE SQUARE.**

2 POINTS

During the Spanish Civil War (1936-1939), 42 people were killed here, victims of a bomb blast. You can still see marks along the wall from the explosion. In the square lies this plaque serving as a memorial to the victims.

SANTA MARIA DEL MAR

This church took only 55 years to build. Only 55 years? Take a look at this place and imagine trying to build it without the machines we have today: no cranes, no bulldozers, no trucks. These machines were to come over 600 years later.

OUTSIDE THE CHURCH

Back in the 1300's, trucks didn't transport the huge stones used to build the church - wagons, animals, and people did.

☐ SCAN THE FRONT DOORS AND LOCATE SYMBOLS OF THE "PORTERS" - PEOPLE WHO TRANSPORTED STONES UPON THEIR BACK.

2 POINTS

13

TOTAL POINTS

- THE PORTERS
- WOODEN BOAT
- COAT-OF-ARMS
- TOMB MARKERS
- STAINED GLASS COLORS

INSIDE THE CHURCH

The banks of the Mediterranean Sea lie but a few minutes from Santa Maria's doors.

Santa Maria del Mar (Saint Mary of the Sea) is the patron saint of sailors. Through the ages Santa Maria seafarers have come here to pray for safe and prosperous journeys.

☐ INSIDE THE CHURCH, TRACK DOWN THIS WOODEN BOAT, A SYMBOL OF SANTA MARIA.

2 POINTS

AGENTS MUST BE ABLE TO SPOT THE
SMALLEST CLUES FROM A DISTANCE. WHEN
YOU'RE ON ASSIGNMENT YOU CAN'T ALWAYS
DEPEND ON BINOCULARS FOR ASSISTANCE,
JUST YOUR OWN TWO EYES.

☐ LOOK UP, EXAMINE THE CEILING, AND
LOCATE THE BARCELONA COAT-OF-ARMS.

3
POINTS

"X" marks the spot – in this case in the shape of a
skull and crossbones indicating the centuries-old
graves lying just beneath your feet.

☐ LOOK DOWN, SCAN THE FLOOR, AND FIND TOMB
MARKERS LIKE THIS ONE.

2
POINTS

In the 1300's (when Santa Maria was built) most people couldn't read. Because of this, images in the form of statues and stained glass windows were used to teach about Christianity. Examine the stained glass and you can make out images of people in the colored glass.

To produce the different shades of glass, craftsmen mixed sand together with wood ash at extremely high temperatures. To create the colors, they added different metals to this mix: copper for green and red, cobalt for blue.

☐ HOW MANY DIFFERENT COLORS CAN YOU FIND IN THE STAINED GLASS?

(1 point per color, 4 points maximum)

SAGRADA FAMÍLIA

(Sagrada Familia = "Sagrada Fah-meal-ee-a")

Spain's most popular monument has been under construction for well over 100 years and is set for completion in 2026.

☐ **FIND A CONSTRUCTION CRANE IN THIS PHOTO.**

1 POINT

- CRANE PHOTO
- ALPHA & OMEGA
- JESUS
- MAGIC SQUARES (2)
- MAGIC SQUARES' NUMBER
- ANGELS' INSTRUMENTS
- SAINT JORDI STATUE
- HOLY FRUIT

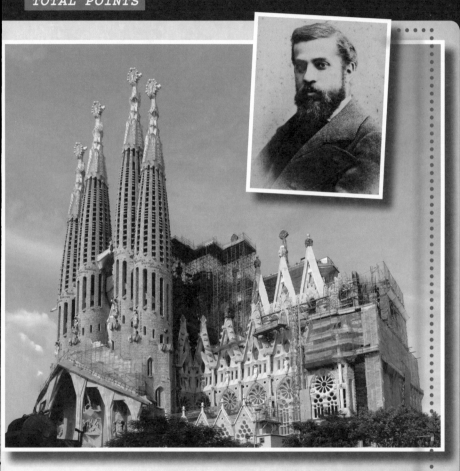

This year (2026) will mark the 100th anniversary of the cathedral's original architect, Antoni Gaudí *("An-toe-nee Gow-dee")*, who lies buried inside the cathedral.

Gaudí filled the cathedral with many symbols. How many can you find?

OUTSIDE THE CATHEDRAL

The "Passion Façade" *(Façade = "Fuh-Sahd")* serves as one of the cathedral entrances. It represents the Passion of Jesus – his pain, sacrifice, and death.

AT THE ENTRANCE FIND:

☐ **THE ALPHA AND OMEGA** ....

1 POINT

Alpha is the Greek symbol for "A" and Omega the symbol for "Z". Together these symbols that represent "A" and "Z" signify the beginning and the end.

2 POINTS

☐ **THE WORD "JESUS" IN THE VERSES OF RELIGIOUS TEXT LINING THE DOORS AND DOORWAY.**

THE "MAGIC SQUARE"

Magic squares have quite a history, popping up in different cultures all over the world, from China to India and countries in the Middle East and Europe. Each is filled with different numbers that have a unique meaning in that particular culture. The first "magic square" appeared around 650 BC in China.

What makes a magic square so "magic"?
In this one, the four numbers forming each row, each column, and the diagonal lines crossing the center add up to the same number.

Test it for yourself. First, add each of the *rows* of four numbers together. Then, add each of the *columns* of four numbers together. Finally, add each of the *diagonals* of four numbers together.

☐ EVERY ROW/COLUMN/DIAGONAL ADDS UP TO **3 POINTS** WHICH NUMBER?

Many think Jesus was this many years old when he died.

☐ EXAMINE THE DOORS LEADING INTO THE
CATHEDRAL AND UNCOVER ANOTHER MAGIC
SQUARE (A GOLD COLOR) HIDDEN IN THE
LINES OF THE DOORWAY TEXT.

The "Nativity Façade" represents the birth of
Jesus. Look above the doorway and find angels
celebrating the birth of Jesus as they play
musical instruments.

2 POINTS

☐ WHAT TWO INSTRUMENTS ARE THE ANGELS
NOT PLAYING?

HARP	PIANO
VIOLIN	DRUMS

INSIDE THE CATHEDRAL

Gaudí designed the inside of the cathedral with beams in the shape of towering trees and the ceiling resembling the treetops. He wanted visitors to feel they were in a forest. Look way up at the ceiling and look around the inside. Use your imagination a bit – do you think Gaudí succeeded in making this space appear like a forest?

☐ **TRACK DOWN THIS STATUE OF SAINT JORDI LOOKING DOWN OVER THE CATHEDRAL VISITORS.**

2
POINTS

Examine the large light hanging over the altar.

☐ **WHAT HOLY FRUIT DANGLES ALONG THE EDGES OF THE LIGHT?**

1
POINT

LA PEDRERA

(Pedrera = "Ped-rare-uh")

Antoni Gaudí, the same architect who designed the Sagrada Familia cathedral, designed this place as a grand residence for one of Barcelona's richest families. Inside you can explore their living quarters, complete with old-fashioned items from the early 1900's.

☐ **LOCATE THESE "HIGH-TECH" GADGETS FROM THE EARLY 20TH CENTURY:**

-**TELEPHONE** **1 POINT**

-**TYPEWRITER** **1 POINT**

WHAT'S THE NAME ON THE TYPEWRITER? **1 POINT**

☐ **EXPLORE THE REST OF THE HOUSE AND FIND THESE:**

-DOOR **1 POINT**

-LA PEDRERA REPLICA **1 POINT**

-CHIMNEY **1 POINT**

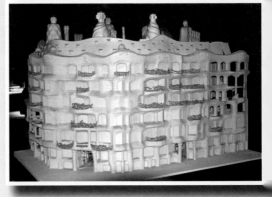

☐ **NEAR LA PEDRERA'S ENTRANCE, HUNT DOWN THIS STREET LAMP.** **2 POINTS**

One of Barcelona's symbols, a bat, hides somewhere in the streetlamp.

☐ **TRACK DOWN THE BAT.** **1 POINT**

JOAN PUJOL GARCIA, A.K.A SECRET AGENT GARBO

(Joan Pujol García = "Jh-wan Puh-jole Gar-see-ah")

Fifteen minutes away from La Pedrera lies a street, Carrer Muntaner *("Kar-air Moon-ta-nair")*, **where one of the greatest double agents* of all time grew up.** Joan Pujol García was a double agent during World War II. Naturally, as a double agent he went by two secret code names. The Nazis (the side he deceived) knew him as **"Arabel."** The British and the Americans (the side he worked for) knew him as **"Garbo."**

Joan Pujol García

Agent Garbo despised everything that the vile Nazis represented. He desperately wanted to see the Allies* defeat them in World War II. So he became a double agent against the Nazis, giving them false intelligence to ensure they didn't win the war. Garbo created a fake identity as one of Spain's strongest Nazi supporters. **He was so crafty that the Nazis wasted no time in recruiting him as a spy and setting him up with cash, invisible ink, and top secret Nazi codes.** Garbo's assignment: spy on the British for the Nazis and recruit more spies. He immediately set off for Britain...or so they thought.

Garbo didn't even set foot in Britain. Instead, he travelled across the Spanish border to Lisbon, Portugal. He got his hands on a few British travel guides, magazines, and movies, and was soon fabricating* spy reports "from Britain." What's more, he pretended to recruit an entire web of over 25 spies – and they didn't even exist. All the while the Nazis were paying him hundreds of thousands of dollars to support his made-up spy ring.

*double agent = an agent pretending to work as a spy for one country but actually working as a spy for that country's enemy

*Allies = The Allies battled the Axis in World War II. The major Allied Powers were the U.S., Britain, France, China, and Russia. The major Axis Powers were Germany (the Nazis), Japan, and Italy.

*fabricating = to "fabricate" means to make up something

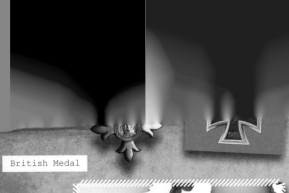

BRITAIN

Normandy Beach

FRANCE

PORTUGAL

SPAIN

Lisbon

Barcelona

SIA

The Nazis totally trusted Garbo, so he began to feed them bogus information about key battles the Allies had in the works. One of these was the invasion of France's Normandy Beach. To cover up the plan, Garbo helped convince the Nazis that the Allies planned to land not at Normandy Beach, but at a different point down the coast. **The Nazis were completely confused, and this made it much easier for the Allies to save Europe and win the war.**

Agent Garbo had the Nazis duped until the very end. **He became one of the only people — if not the only person — to receive medals from both sides during World War II.** He received a medal from the British as Agent Garbo. The Nazis, never suspecting a thing, awarded him a medal as Agent Arabel. After the war, though, the truth came out. Pujol, fearing for his life, fled to the African nation of Angola where he faked his own death. He then escaped to the South American country of Venezuela where he lived a quiet life managing a gift shop.

CASA BATLLÓ

(Casa Batlló= "Kah-sah Bah-tee-oh")

This place is also known as the *Casa Dels Ossos* (House of Bones), thanks to its skeleton-like appearance. It's also known as the *Casa Del Drac* (House of the Dragon). Examine the outside and you can see traces of this Barcelona symbol – a dragon's scales represented by the multi-colored tiles and a dragon's back represented by the curving shape of the roof.

☐ **LOOK TOWARDS THE ROOF AND LOCATE THE ROUNDED STEEPLE AND CROSS.**   **2 POINTS**

Some say that these represent the sword Saint Jordi used to stab the dragon, thereby saving the princess and townspeople from the evil beast.

☐ **NEAR CASA BATLLÓ'S ENTRANCE, HUNT DOWN A STREETLAMP LIKE THIS ONE (THE SAME STYLE AS THE ONE FOUND NEAR LA PEDRERA).**   **2 POIN**

☐ **WHAT ANIMAL RESTS AT**   **1 POINT**
THE TOP OF THE STREETLAMP?

- CASA BATLLÓ'S STEEPLE AND CROSS
- STREETLAMP, ANIMAL AT THE TOP
- CASA AMATLLER'S SAINT JORDI SCULPTURE
- CASA LLEÓ MORERA'S DRAGONS AND BAT SIGN

TOTAL POINTS

If you face Casa Batlló, to the left stands Casa Amatller *(Amatller = Ah-maht-yer)*, a mansion built for a wealthy chocolate merchant.

☐ **SCAN THE FRONT TO DISCOVER THE STATUE OF SAINT JORDI BATTLING THE INFAMOUS DRAGON.**

2 POINTS

From Casa Amatller, continue up the street (away from Casa Batlló) to reach another "casa": Casa Lleó Morera *(Lleó Morera = "Yo More-air-ah")* at the end of the block. Dragons and bats await here as well.

☐ **UNCOVER AT LEAST 10 DRAGONS PERCHED ALONG THE OUTSIDE.**
2 POINTS

☐ **TRACK DOWN THIS SIGN AND IN IT FIND A BAT.**
2 POINTS

PARC DE LA CIUTADELLA

(Parc de la Ciutadella = "Park duh la See-oo-tah-dell-ah")

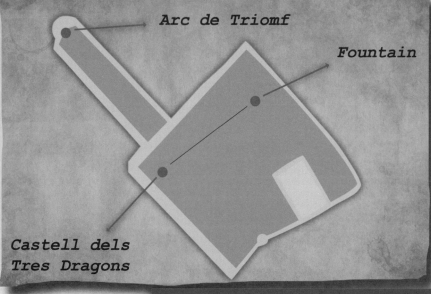

Arc de Triomf

Fountain

Castell dels
Tres Dragons

Parc de la Ciutadella Map

SECRET AGENTS MUST HAVE FIRST-RATE SKILLS WHEN IT COMES TO ANALYZING MAPS. Put yours to the test as you uncover these locations in Parc de la Ciutadella - and discover even more of the city's symbols.

☐ **MAKE YOUR WAY TO THE FOUNTAIN WITH A WATERFALL.**

2 POINTS

☐ **LOCATE FOUR DRAGONS IN THE FOUNTAIN.**

1 POINT

11

TOTAL POINTS

- FOUNTAIN, FOUR DRAGONS
- CASTELL DELS TRES DRAGONS, MORE DRAGONS
- ARC DE TRIOMF, COAT-OF-ARMS, CITY SYMBOL, BATS

☐ **FIND YOUR WAY TO CASTELL DELS TRES DRAGONS.**
("Ka-stel Dels Trez Dra-gohns")
(Three Dragons Castle in English)

 2 POINTS

☐ **UNCOVER THE DRAGONS WALKING ALONG THE EDGE OF A FOUNTAIN WITH THEIR TONGUES STICKING OUT.**

1 POINT

☐ **VENTURE TO THE ARC DE TRIOMF.**
("Ark duh Tree-omf")

2 POINTS

☐ **FIND THE CITY'S COAT OF ARMS IN THE ARCH AND ON THE POLES BESIDE THE ARCH.**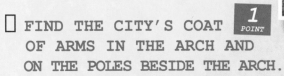

1 POINT

☐ **WHAT ANIMAL RESTS AT THE VERY TOP OF THE POLES?**

1 POINT

☐ **TRACK DOWN THE BATS.**
(Hint: they're somewhere on the arch.)

1 POINT

PARC GÜELL

("Parc Güell = Park Gway")

**THE BEST SECRET AGENTS HAVE KEEN MEMORIES
– REMEMBERING KEY DETAILS THAT THE REST
OF US USUALLY FORGET. NOW IT'S TIME TO
TEST YOUR MEMORY.**

The same architect who designed Sagrada Familia
cathedral, La Pedrera, and Casa Batlló designed
this park.

☐ **WHO'S THE ARCHITECT?**
1 POINT

Colorful mosaics fill this whimsical park. (A
"mosaic" is an image made of small pieces of
colored glass or colored stone.) Hunt down these
mosaics:

☐ **THE "PARK GÜELL" SIGN**
2 POINTS ·················

(Notice that 'park' is in English, not Catalan.)

7

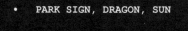

TOTAL POINTS

☑ **ONE OF THE CITY SYMBOLS: A DRAGON**

2 POINTS

(This time it resembles a giant lizard.)

☐ **THE SUN**

2 POINTS

(Keep your head up for this one.)

53

CASTELL DE MONTJUÏC

(Castell de Montjuïc = Kastell duh Mohn-jhoo-eek)

Castell de Montjuïc ("Montjuïc Castle") sits proudly atop the mountain of Montjuïc. A fortress has stood at this prime spot for almost 400 years. Need the perfect location to keep watch over the city, the port, and the sea? This is it. A system of protective walls, moats, cannons, and guns surrounds the fortress, guarding Barcelona from above.

LOCATE A CITY LOOKOUT POINT AND FIND THESE:

☐ **SAGRADA FAMILIA CATHEDRAL** **1** POINT

☐ **A CRUISE SHIP** **1** POINT

11

TOTAL POINTS

ON THE CASTLE GROUNDS, TRACK DOWN:

☐ TWO CANNONS   **2** POINTS

☐ THE GUARD STATION   **2** POINTS

☐ TAKE YOUR POST INSIDE   **2** POINTS
AND HAVE YOUR PHOTO SNAPPED
"STANDING GUARD."

☐ THE OLD-FASHIONED   **2** POINTS
"CLOCK" (ALSO KNOW AS A
SUNDIAL)

☐ WHAT YEAR WAS THE   **1** POINT
SUNDIAL CARVED INTO THE
STONE? 17_ _

TOP-NOTCH AGENTS HAVE A HIGH LEVEL OF SOMETHING CALLED "SITUATIONAL AWARENESS." THESE SHARP AGENTS PAY CLOSE ATTENTION TO THEIR SURROUNDINGS – READY, AT A MOMENT'S NOTICE, TO COLLECT VITAL INTELLIGENCE AND TO ESCAPE FROM DANGEROUS SITUATIONS. HAVING EXCELLENT "SITUATIONAL AWARENESS" (SA FOR SHORT) MEANS ALWAYS REMAINING "ON ALERT."

These missions test your SA. You can complete these at any time during your stay. Remain "on alert" as you wander around Barcelona, or else you'll miss chances to win points.

SPANISH FOOD

To properly blend in, you'll need to eat Spanish food. In a foreign country nothing blows your cover more than eating only hamburgers and french fries.

EARN 1 POINT FOR EACH OF THESE YOU TRY.

my notes:
_____
_____

 PATATAS BRAVAS **1 POINT**
(*"Puh-tah-tahs Brahv-ahs"*)
(Fried potatoes with a yummy sauce)

 TORTILLA **1 POINT**
(Totally different from Mexican tortillas, these are similar to potato omelettes.)

☐ **MANCHEGO CHEESE** **1 POINT**
(*"Mahn-chay-go"*) (A special kind of Spanish cheese)

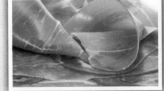

☐ **SPANISH HAM** **1 POINT**
(In Spain, people love this stuff!)

 CREMA CATALANA **1 POINT**
(*"Krema Kaht-ah-lahn-a"*)(A creamy custard topped with a layer of sweet, crunchy caramel)

☑ **CHOCOLATE AND CHURROS**

1 POINT

(Donut sticks dipped in thick hot chocolate)

☐ **HORCHATA** *("Or-chah-tah")* **1** POINT
(A cold drink made from water, sugar, and nuts ground together so finely that the texture resembles milk)

STREET MUSICIANS

Look *and* listen especially around La Rambla and Barri Gòtic for street musicians serenading you with their melodies.

☑ **ONE POINT FOR EACH STREET MUSICIAN YOU SPOT.** **3** POINTS
(3 points max)

To receive each point, you must also name the instrument played.

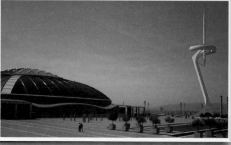

BARCELONA OLYMPIC SOUVENIRS

In 1992 Barcelona hosted the Summer Olympic Games. Find the Olympic rings in various forms around the city, serving as reminders of the event. The rings could be on a building, on a flag, or in the form of a souvenir.

Barcelona '92

☑ **1 POINT FOR EACH SET OF RINGS FOUND**
   (3 points max)

3
POINTS

FC BARCELONA SOUVENIRS

It's impossible to visit Barcelona without stumbling upon souvenirs from the city's soccer team – FC Barcelona. Movies have been made about this legendary team. If you want to get in big trouble in Barcelona, tell a local that you're a fan of FC Barcelona's staunch rival – Madrid.

Track down these souvenirs with the FC Barcelona logo.

☑ **SOCCER JERSEY**   **1** POINT

☑ **SOCCER BALL**   **1** POINT

ANSWER KEY

Once an answer is submitted, your case officer can check it here.

If you peek at this answer key before submitting a final answer, you won't receive any points for that clue. Most clues do not have one correct answer, for those that do, here are the answers.

-Pre-Arrival Brief

#1 La Rambla
-Plaça de Catalunya : The statue at Plaça de Catalunya holds a ship. Frederic Marès sculpted it.
-Canaletes Fountain: "B" is the city coat-of-arms.
-Portaferrissa Fountain: The animals in the fountain: dog, horse, bird
-The Boqueria: Items not in the Boqueria sign: Image of Saint Jordi, Spain's flag
-Casa Bruno Cuadros: A fan is beside the dragon and on the building walls.
-Mosaic: Joan Miró created the mosaic.
-Plaça Reial: Saint Jordi's crosses are on the streetlamp.

#2 Port Vell: Columbus Statue: An anchor (the symbol of the sea) is between the two words.

#3 La Catedral: The courtyard birds: geese.

#4 Plaça Nova: The Romans called Barcelona "Barcino."
-A crown was added to the horse.

#7 Sagrada Família: The crane is on the left side of the photo.
-Every row/column/diagonal adds up to 33.
-The instruments the angels are not playing: piano, drums.
-The holy fruit dangling along the light's edges: grapes.

#8 La Pedrera: The name on the typewriter: Underwood

#9 Casa Batlló: The animal resting atop the streetlamp: a bat

#10 Parc de la Ciutadella: The animal resting at the top of the poles: a dragon

#11 Parc Güell: The architect: Antoni Gaudí

#12 Castell de Montjuïc: The sundial was carved in 1777.

THE FINAL MISSION

Case officers, please visit
scavengerhuntadventures.com/hunt
(all lowercase letters)

☐ **SIGN UP FOR OUR EMAIL LIST TO GET:**

• *The Museum Spy*: a free e-book

• A chance to win a **personalized copy** of any of our books printed especially for your agent (and even more **free** books!); Details online.

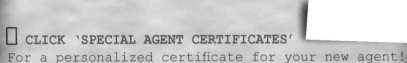

☐ **CLICK 'SPECIAL AGENT CERTIFICATES'** For a personalized certificate for your new agent!

GREAT FOR GROUP TRIPS

We offer **special multi-copy pricing** and **personalized books** - great for field trips and group trips. Visit **scavengerhuntadventures.com/groups** for more info.

PLEASE HELP SPREAD THE WORD

We're a small family business and would be thrilled if you **left a review online*** or recommended our books to a friend.

OUR BOOKS
Paris, London, Amsterdam, Rome, New York, D.C., Barcelona, St. Augustine - more on the way!

...an't mention the site name here, but it begins with "AM"!

All images are from BigStock.Com unless listed below. The two digit numbers are the file license number (links below), links to Flickr photographer sites are also below. License for all Flickr photos is Creative Commons 2.0. (T=Top, B=Bottom, M=Middle; L=Left, R=Right, C=Center); FROM WIKIPEDIA: p.4:NASA; p.7:Heralder-3.0;p.11: T-1997-3.0;p.8&9:Ajuntament Palma;p.12-R-Haitham Alfalah-3.0;p.13-T-Enfo-3.0; B-Heralder-3.0;p.14-Enfo-3.0;p.15-Bocachete;p.16-T-Stanislav Kozlovskiy-3.0, B (Both)- Heralder-3.0;p.17-T-Tony Hisgett-2.0;p.18-TL-Josep Renalias-2.0;p.21-B-David Iliff (www. facebook.com/diliff)-3.0;p.22:R-Metropolitan Museum of Art;p.23-T-Selby May; B-Fabio Alessandro Locati-3.0;p.24-TL-Bohringer Friedrich (rufre@lenz-nenning.at)-2.5; TR-Mutari;p.27-B-JoJan-3.0;TR-Magí Pujadas;p.29-TR-Pablo Audouard Deglaire;p.30 & p.31-TR-Xavier Caballe-2.0;p.32-TR-Pere Lopez-3.0;p.33-B-Pere Lopez-3.0; T-Enfo-3.0;p.34-T & p.35-T &p.36-T: PMRMaeyart-3.0;p.36-B-Enfo-3.0;p.39-Bernard Gagnon;p.40-L-JoJan-3.0; R-Etan Tal-3.0;p.40-B-Don Vip-3.0;p.41-Tony Hisgett-2.0;p.42-BR-Wiki Ktulu-3.0;p.43-B-Sagrada Familia-3.0;p.45-MR-Tony Hisgett-2.0;p.48-TR-Bernard Gagnon-3.0;p.49-TL-Year of the Dragon-3.0;p.49-BR-Mutari;p.50-Bernard Gagnon-3.0;p.51:T-Selby May-3.0;M-Amaia Hodge;p.52-R & p.53-BR-Delia Lendeczki;p.53-C-Bernard Gagnon;p.54-T-Oleg Kalimov;p.54-BR-Matt Wade (http://en.wikipedia.org/wiki/User:UpstateNYer); p.55-T-Eric Chan-2.0;MR-Alf Van Beem-1.0; p.61-T-Louvre;B-Art Institute of Chicago; FROM FLICKR: p.25-M. Peinado; p.28-L-Helga Lobster Stew; p.32-TL-Matilde Martinez; B-Jorapa; p.34-B and p. 37-Ferran Pestana; p.42-T-Hammershaug; p.44-T-Craig Cormack; p.44-MR-Andrew Fogg; BR-Alejandro Moreno Calvo; p.45-T-TW Buckner; B-Wenjie Zhang; p.48-B-Wenjie Zhang;p.49-BL-Kwong Yee Cheng;p.53-T-Javier Vito;p.55-ML-Sharon Mollerus;B-Bobo Boom; Flickr User Page Links: Alejandro Calvo: almorca/; Andrew Fogg: 69024001@N00; Bobo Boom: fotnmc; Craig Cormack: craigyc; Ferran Pestana: ferranp; Hammershaug: 26777097@N03; Helga Lobster Stew: lobsterstew; Javier Vito: jparigini/; Jorapa: jorapa; Kwong Yee Cheng: 98153629@N00; M. Peinado: mpeinadopa/; Matilde Martinez: 25039539@N05; Sharon Mollerus: clairity; TW Buckner: twbuckner; Wenjie Zhang: z_wenjie; FLICKR LICENSE 2.0 (all Flickr Images): http://creativecommons.org/licenses/by/2.0/; WIKIMEDIA LICENSE LINKS (2.0-3.5): http://creativecommons.org/ licenses/by/2.0/, http://creativecommons.org/licenses/by/2.5/, http://creativecommons.org/licenses/by/3.0.